"Biological diversity is messy. It walks, it crawls, it swims, it swoops, it buzzes. But extinction is silent and it has no voice other than our own."

Paul Hawken, American environmentalist

www.mascotbooks.com

Can We Save Them? An Alphabet of Species in Danger

For more information, please contact
Mascot Books, an imprint of Amplify Publishing Group
620 Herndon Parkway, Suite 320
Herndon, VA 20170
info@mascotbooks.com

Library of Congress Control Number: 2022908110

CPSIA Code: PRV0522A
ISBN-13: 978-1-63755-346-6

Printed in the United States

Can We Save Them?

An Alphabet of Species in Danger

Written and Illustrated by
Vicki Malone

This book spotlights just twenty-six of the thousands of living things that are in trouble—endangered because of human beings. Habitat loss, climate change, pesticides, insecticides, wars, and poaching are a few of the contributing factors.

Jane Goodall, the famous primatologist, calls the earth a living tapestry. Everything that lives is threaded into it.

When too many threads are pulled, the tapestry unravels.

Humans are realizing that we are not separated from this tapestry; rather, we are also threads in it. So what can we do? As a first step, we can learn about some of the many animals and plants currently threatened with extinction. This knowledge can inspire action and hope.

And there is hope. In the United States the Endangered Species Act—along with many dedicated individuals and organizations—helped save the bald eagle, peregrine falcon, gray whale, and grizzly bear from extinction.

People around the world are working to keep our beautiful tapestry intact.

The International Union for Conservation of Nature (IUCN) Red List of Threatened Species and reports from the United States Fish and Wildlife Service and Vermont Fish and Wildlife Service are used in this book.

Asian Elephant *Elephas maximus indicus*

In the Hindu religion the Asian elephant is a sacred animal. The elephant represents Lord Ganesh, who has wisdom and is the remover of all obstacles. That fairly describes an elephant!

Asian elephants are intelligent, have distinct personalities, and form close relationships with others in their herd. They show sadness and grief when one of their herd dies. They weigh as much as eleven thousand pounds and have an incredible sense of smell. Their long, versatile trunks can lift a heavy fallen tree or gently pick up a single peanut!

Why is the Asian elephant important? It is a key animal in its habitat. Its dung spreads seeds and fertilizes the soil. It has been important in Asian cultures and religions for many centuries.

Why is it in trouble? It is at risk due to habitat loss and deadly conflicts with humans because of property and agriculture destruction. Countries are making efforts to protect Asian elephants by creating preserves and helping farmers protect their crops.

Where does it live? India and Southeast Asia

Endangered Status: Critically endangered (IUCN)

Blue Whale *Balaenoptera musculus*

The blue whale is the largest animal in the world. An adult blue whale is as long as a basketball court. But this behemoth lives on a diet of tiny ocean creatures—little shrimp-like animals called krill. The blue whale has no teeth and eats krill by filtering them through fringed plates in its mouth—up to forty million krill a day!

Blue whales communicate with each other using complex sounds that can be heard underwater from many miles away.

Why is the blue whale important? It is at the top of the ocean food chain and keeps the number of krill and phytoplankton in balance for the health of the ocean.

Why is it in trouble? Ocean noise, pollution, injuries from ships, and fewer krill because of warming oceans due to climate change have greatly reduced the blue whale population.

Where does it live? All oceans
Endangered Status: Endangered (IUCN)

Common Seahorse *Hippocampus kuda*

The common seahorse is a very surprising creature! It is a fish, even though it does not look like one. It has skin over bony plates instead of scales, no teeth, and no stomach. It also has a tail like a monkey and a face that looks like . . . well, a horse.

But the most amazing thing about the seahorse is that the male gives birth to the babies instead of the female! He has a pouch where the female drops eggs for him to fertilize. Between twenty and twenty-eight days later, usually under a full moon, the male gives birth to between one and two hundred fully-formed tiny seahorses.

Why is the common seahorse important? It helps keep the ocean ecosystem in balance.

Why is it in trouble? Habitat loss, pollution, being accidentally caught in fishing nets, and being sold as tourist trinkets are its greatest risks.

Where does it live? Shallow waters of the Pacific and Indian Oceans
Endangered Status: Vulnerable (IUCN)

Dogwood *Cornus florida*

The delicate white flowers of the dogwood tree signal that spring has come to the forest. Many animals eat its bark and leaves. Bears, chipmunks, and birds love the high-fat red dogwood berries.

Why is the dogwood tree important? Besides being a valuable food source, the dogwood plays a very important role in adding calcium to the forest. Calcium is essential for animals and plants. Unlike most other plants, the dogwood can absorb calcium directly from soil and rocks. Then its fallen leaves and bark provide calcium in a digestible form for animals and other plants. Calcium is vital for healthy birds' eggs, strong snail shells, and a better forest environment.

Why is it in trouble? The deadly, invasive anthracnose dogwood fungus was introduced to North America in the 1970s. This fungus is found throughout the dogwood's habitat.

Where does it live? Eastern North America

Endangered Status: Threatened in Vermont (Vermont Fish & Wildlife Service)

Ethiopian Wolf *Canis simensis*

The Ethiopian wolf looks more like a big red coyote. It only roams Ethiopia's high mountains, and has evolved to survive the harsh environment of cold winters and very little water. Today, few Ethiopian wolves remain, but scientists are not sure of the number.

This wolf is the top predator in its habitat. They live together in packs, and mother wolves share in raising each other's pups. But the wolves hunt alone, catching rats and mice.

Why is the Ethiopian wolf important? It controls the number of rodents in its environment.

Why is it in trouble? Habitat loss and diseases like rabies and distemper from domestic dogs have decimated the population. But there are now programs to vaccinate dogs and wolves to protect them from these diseases. This is helping both the animals and humans!

Where does it live? A few mountains in Ethiopia, Africa

Endangered status: Endangered (IUCN)

Florida Scrub-Jay *Aphelocoma coerulescens*

The Florida scrub-jay is a real Florida native who lives in parts of the state with sandy areas and low-growing oak shrubs.

These beautiful twelve-inch birds are smart and have astonishing memories. Each will bury six to nine thousand acorns in the sand and mark each place with a pebble or twig. More than half are recovered and eaten later during the winter. Humans would probably not be as successful! They also eat insects, toads, and mice.

Florida scrub-jays are brash and curious, and they may decide to land on your head to get a closer look at you!

Why is the Florida scrub-jay important? It has lived in this small part of the world for over two million years and is found nowhere else on earth. It is an essential part of its ecosystem.

Why is it in trouble? It is vulnerable due to fragmentation of habitat causing a lack of genetic diversity and habitat loss.

Where does it live? Florida
Endangered status: Vulnerable (IUCN)

Golden Frog (Panamanian) *Atelopus zeteki*

This tiny frog's bright color announces, "Poisonous! Do not eat me." When a male golden frog sees a potential mate, he waves his arms at her. If she likes him, she waves back!

Why is the golden frog important? Like all amphibians, it provides an early indicator of environmental changes. Because amphibians breathe partly through their skin, they are very sensitive to pollution, diseases, and toxins. Amphibians give an early warning that their environment is in trouble.

The golden frog is no longer found anywhere in its habitat. Scientists believe it has been extinct in the wild since 2006. So what happened?

Why is it in trouble? Like too many amphibians around the world, golden frogs were killed by the chytrid fungus that spreads through water. Now golden frogs are found only in zoos and laboratories that are free from the fungus. Hopefully they can be safely released into the wild one day.

Where does it live? Extinct in the wild

Endangered status: Critically endangered (IUCN)

Hawksbill Sea Turtle *Eretmochelys imbricata*

This turtle is called "hawksbill" because its mouth looks a lot like a bird's beak—all the better to get inside the little nooks and crannies in coral to eat sea sponges.

A hawksbill sea turtle can live for fifty years, and the female lays her first eggs when she is between twenty-five and thirty years old. When she is ready, she finds a quiet sandy beach and digs a hole with her flippers. She lays about one hundred and fifty eggs and covers them with sand before going back to the sea. After two months the hatchling turtles dig out of the sand and make their way to the ocean. It is a dangerous journey because they are vulnerable to predators like seagulls and crabs. If they make it to the water, the female turtles know exactly where to lay their eggs many years later—the beach where they were born!

Why is the hawksbill turtle important? They keep the sea sponge population in check, which helps coral reefs.

Why is it in trouble? It has been badly affected by dying coral reefs due to climate change, habitat loss for laying eggs, and getting caught in fishing nets. Illegal use of their shells for jewelry also occurs.

Where does it live? Tropical and subtropical oceans

Endangered status: Critically endangered (IUCN)

Ivory-Billed Woodpecker *Campephilus principallus*

This woodpecker is large and beautiful. It drills with its big bill into dead trees to find beetle larvae.

Some ornithologists insist this bird has been extinct since 1944, and others say, "No way!" But for a woodpecker with a thirty-inch wingspan, it has been extremely hard to find. Maybe one was seen in Florida in 1950, Texas in 1968, Arkansas in 2004, Louisiana in 2006, and Florida in 2007. But then again, maybe not. One photo taken in 1971 that was believed to show the woodpecker turned out to be a stuffed bird in a tree!

Why is the ivory-billed woodpecker important? The tree cavities it makes are used by other species such as blue birds, honeybees, opossums, and squirrels.

Why is it in trouble? It could once be found in many areas of the southern United States, but suffered major habitat loss due to years of forest destruction and mining.

Where does it live? East Texas to Florida

Endangered status: Critically endangered (IUCN); declared extinct by the US Fish and Wildlife Service in 2021

Japanese Red-Crowned Crane *Grus japonensis*

The Japanese red-crowned crane is a beautiful dancer! These five-foot tall birds leap, bow, and bob their heads gracefully in their courtship dance. When one finds a mate, they stay together for life. Red-crowned cranes nest and feed in deep water marshes and have very long, sharp bills to spear fish, frogs, and rodents.

In Japanese culture, this crane represents happiness, long life, and good luck. Children in Japan learn how to fold paper into the shape of the crane. This paper folding art is called origami.

Why is the Japanese red-crowned crane important? It symbolizes luck and love to many people, and is very important in Japanese culture. It controls rodent and insect populations.

Why is it in trouble? Habitat loss due to agriculture, loss of forests, and road building have decimated its population.

Where does it live? China, Japan, Korea
Endangered status: Endangered (IUCN)

Key Deer *Odocoileus virginianus clavium*

When the last ice age ended about ten thousand years ago, glaciers melted and oceans rose. White-tailed deer living in the southern ridge of land now called Florida found themselves on islands isolated from the mainland. These islands are the Florida Keys.

Interesting things happen when a large mammal lives on an island. It usually becomes smaller to better utilize the island's resources—and that is just what the Key deer did! An adult white-tailed deer can weigh up to three hundred pounds, but the little Key deer weighs only forty-five to seventy-five pounds.

Why is the Key deer important? The Key deer is an important part of the Florida Keys' ecosystem and has adapted itself to the different habitats of the Keys. Residents of the Keys consider these small deer national treasures.

Why is it in trouble? Habitat loss and death by vehicles and dogs have put it at risk. Today, underpasses and fencing are being built to protect the deer.

Where does it live? Only a few of the Florida Keys

Endangered status: Endangered (IUCN)

Lemur (Ring-Tailed) *Lemur catta*

All lemurs are primates, just like monkeys and apes, and the ring-tailed lemur only lives in the wild on the African island of Madagascar.

The male does something rather obnoxious when defending his territory or challenging other males for a mate—it STINK FIGHTS! He rubs his tail with the smelly secretions from scent glands on his wrists and waves his tail in his adversary's face. The most stinky lemur wins!

Unlike other lemurs that live in trees, the ring-tailed spends a lot of time on the ground. It eats small vertebrates, plants, and insects, and it especially loves tamarind pods and leaves.

This lemur's tail is longer than its body. When traveling in a group, they raise their tails like flags to keep the conspiracy (the name for a group of lemurs) together.

Why is the ring-tailed lemur important? It eats fruit and plants and excretes the seeds onto the forest floor. This helps the forest grow.

Why is it in trouble? All one hundred and ten subspecies of lemurs are endangered due to habitat loss.

Where does it live? Madagascar
Endangered status: Endangered (IUCN)

Mountain Gorilla *Gorilla beringei beringei*

We are closely related to gorillas, having a whopping 98 percent of overlapping genetic codes. Gorillas laugh, cry, grieve, think about the past and future, and can make tools. People have even been able to teach gorillas raised in captivity to communicate using American Sign Language!

The mountain gorilla has longer, thicker hair than other gorilla subspecies, because it can get very cold in the mountains. They eat leaves, bark, fruit, and insects, and can weigh as much as four hundred pounds. They live in troops headed by a dominant male, called a silverback, who is father to most of the gorilla babies.

Why is the mountain gorilla important? It eats lots of vegetation, which helps keep its habitat in balance.

Why is it in trouble? Habitat loss, wars, human diseases, and naturally low birthrates are major factors. The mountain gorilla, however, is the only gorilla subspecies whose numbers have increased! This is because of effective conservation efforts led by countries and organizations.

Where does it live? Mountains in areas of Rwanda, Uganda, Democratic Republic of Congo

Endangered status: Endangered (IUCN)

Numbat *Myrmecobius fasciatus*

A numbat is a termite's worst nightmare. This little Australian marsupial eats only termites and can consume up to twenty thousand a day! To slurp up termites, the numbat has a very long, sticky tongue that is half the length of its twenty-four-inch body. It also has a long, pointed nose for getting into holes and logs in search of the insects. A numbat gets all the water it needs from eating termites.

Numbats live in Australian eucalyptus forests where fallen trees provide for their nesting and food. Female numbats give birth to about four babies the size of jellybeans. Blind when born, they stay in their mother's skinfold, which acts like a pouch, for six to seven months.

Why is the numbat important? It controls the termite population of its habitat.

Why is it in trouble? It is at risk due to habitat loss, fires, and being killed by foxes and domestic cats.

Where does it live? Southwestern Australia

Endangered status: Endangered (IUCN)

Ostrich (Somali) *Struthio molybdophanes*

The ostrich is an amazing bird! It cannot fly, but the male ostrich can roar like a lion. He can be heard from several miles away and is telling other males, "Keep out of my territory!" And ostriches do NOT stick their heads in the sand—how could they breathe? They do dig a hole in the sand to lay their eggs, and both males and females look in that hole and guard them.

An ostrich is the world's biggest bird at six to nine feet tall. They can run up to forty-five miles per hour—in fact, they are the fastest runners on two legs. And if necessary, those strong, clawed legs can kill an adult lion! Their diet is plants, insects, and reptiles.

Why is the ostrich important? The ostrich has been an important part of its ecosystem for millions of years.

Why is it in trouble? Not all are in trouble, but this subspecies is suffering from habitat loss and is killed for its meat and feathers.

Where does it live? Northeast Africa
Endangered status: Vulnerable (IUCN)

Polar Bear *Ursus maritimus*

The polar bear's Latin name, *Ursus maritimus,* means "sea bear." It is an apt name because a polar bear spends most of its life near the sea, in the sea, and especially on sea ice. It relies on sea ice to hunt, rest, breed, and raise its cubs.

Polar bears need to eat lots of fat to survive the very cold weather. They swim at six miles per hour to catch bearded and ringed seals— their favorite meals. They are the world's largest bears, weighing up to twelve hundred pounds. Polar bears have black skin, white fur, a blue tongue and a four-inch layer of body fat!

Why is the polar bear important? It is at the top of the Arctic food chain and keeps the ecosystem in balance. Its presence is a sign of a healthy environment.

Why is it in trouble? As climate change increases the temperature of the oceans, sea ice—the polar bear's prime habitat—is disappearing. Unless climate change is lessened, scientists predict the polar bear will be headed for extinction by the end of this century.

Where does it live? Arctic Circle

Endangered status: Vulnerable (IUCN)

Queen Alexandra's Birdwing *Ornithoptera alexandrae*

Fluttering high in the tropical forests of Papua New Guinea is the largest butterfly in the world. The magnificent blue, green, and red male Queen Alexandra's birdwing is also considered the world's most beautiful butterfly! The male has a wingspan of about seven inches, while the brown female is a huge twelve inches.

Very little is understood about this butterfly because its life is spent high in the tree canopy where it lays eggs and feeds on flowering vines. It was first seen by Europeans in 1907 and is named after Queen Alexandra of Great Britain.

Why is Queen Alexandra's birdwing important? It is an important part of its ecosystem. If one species goes extinct, its whole environment suffers.

Why is it in trouble? It suffers from habitat loss from logging and agriculture, as well as illegal catching and selling.

Where does it live? Small area of Papua New Guinea

Endangered status: Endangered (IUCN)

Rusty Patched Bumble Bee *Bombus affinus*

Do you like tomatoes, peppers, or cranberries? If so, thank a bumble bee! The pollen of those plants is hard to get, and only the bumble bee has developed a way to extract it. She grabs hold of the flower with her jaws and vibrates her whole body, and out flies the pollen. Most of the pollen goes into a "pollen basket" on her hind legs to feed the colony, but some of it will stay on her body to fertilize the next plant she lands on.

She is a good flyer in all kinds of weather, even when she is loaded down with the nectar and pollen that can more than double her weight. This has scientists amazed!

Why is the rusty patched bumble bee important? It is a critical pollinator of flowers, fruits, and vegetables.

Why is it in trouble? Many bumble bees are in trouble because of diseases, pesticides, and habitat loss. We can help them by growing native plants and eliminating neonicotinoid pesticides on lawns and gardens.

Where does it live? Eastern North America and upper Midwest

Endangered status: Critically endangered (ICUN)

Sea Otter *Enhydra lutris*

In the ocean, above kelp forests, a sea otter glides on its back and uses a rock to smash the shells of sea urchins, shellfish, and crabs for a tasty meal. Sea otters are one of just a few mammals that use tools.

Sea otters can live in very cold water because they have incredibly dense fur to protect them. But that fur needs to be groomed and cleaned regularly to maintain its insulating ability.

Why is the sea otter important? It is a top predator in its ecosystems. It keeps the number of sea urchins down, which protects kelp. This helps other marine animals who depend on the kelp for protection and food.

Why is it in trouble? It was hunted to near extinction for its fur before an international treaty was signed in 1911. Today, pollution, parasites, infectious disease, oil spills, and kelp loss endanger the sea otter.

Where does it live? Pacific coast of Russia, Alaska to Vancouver Island, central California coast

Endangered status: Endangered (IUCN)

Tiger *Panthera tigris*

Tigers are awesome! This big cat is popular in zoos, and it has been featured in books, movies, TV shows, cartoons, and even breakfast cereal.

Tigers live in Asia and are the world's biggest cats, weighing up to six hundred and sixty pounds. With large padded feet, they silently stalk their prey—animals like antelope, wild pigs, and water buffalo. Their ferocious roars can be heard from two miles away. Tigers can run forty miles per hour and, unlike your pet kitty, they love to swim. Just like our fingerprints, no two tigers' stripes are exactly alike.

Why is the tiger important? The tiger is the top predator in its environment and keeps its prey population under control and its habitat healthy.

Why is it in trouble? It suffers from habitat loss, illegal killing for body parts used in questionable medical practices, and contact with humans. In one hundred years their numbers have decreased by 70 percent. But there is hope! India and Nepal's tiger populations are increasing because of government tiger preserves.

Where does it live? Southwest Asia, Sumatra, North Korea, China, India, Nepal, Siberia

Endangered status: Six subspecies Endangered and three subspecies Extinct (IUCN)

Utah Prairie Dog *Cynomys parvidens*

The Utah prairie dog is the smallest in size of all five prairie dog species. A prairie dog is a burrowing squirrel that lives in colonies of family groups in the Great Plains and desert grasslands of North America.

They build elaborate tunnel homes with underground rooms for sleeping, raising young, and storing food—and they even have toilets! Their diet is grass, flowers, and seeds. The Utah prairie dog has a sophisticated communication system of yips that tells their colony exactly what kind of predator is coming. They can even describe a human with a gun!

Why is the Utah prairie dog important? Its burrows are also home to rabbits, snakes, spiders, and other animals that cannot dig homes for themselves. It is also a primary food source for hawks, coyotes, foxes, and critically endangered black-footed ferrets.

Why is it in trouble? In the past it was killed because its burrows interfered with farms and ranches. It has also been affected by disease and drought. Many have been relocated to safer public lands.

Where does it live? Southwest Utah

Endangered status: Endangered (IUCN)

Venus Flytrap *Dionaea muscipula*

The Venus flytrap has the wrong name. This amazing flower captures ants, spiders, and other crawling insects, but hardly any flies! It grows in poor, acidic soil, and has evolved to get necessary nutrients by digesting insects.

This carnivorous plant has a very clever way of getting a meal and seems to know how to count. If an insect wanders into its two-lobed, prickly leaves and touches two of those prickly extensions within two seconds, only then will the leaf snap shut to trap the bug. It then exudes some digestive juices, and dinner is served!

But insects must pollinate the Venus flytrap flower. That problem is solved because the flower stem rises high above the leaf traps and is pollinated by flying beetles and sweat bees.

Why is the Venus flytrap important? It is one of the most recognized and loved plants and is an important tourist attraction in its native North and South Carolina.

Why is it in trouble? It is vulnerable due to habitat loss and poaching.

Where does it live? Small areas of North and South Carolina
Endangered status: Vulnerable (IUCN)

Western Lily *Lilium occidentale*

The western lily is quite beautiful. To see its red blossoms bobbing in the wind is a rare and wonderful sight. The lily is now very hard to find in its home among the coastal grasslands and bogs of northern California and southern Oregon.

Why is the western lily important? It has been part of its coastal ecosystem for thousands of years and produces more nectar for pollinators, especially hummingbirds, than any other American lily.

Why is it in trouble? Because of its beauty, many western lilies have been taken by collectors over the years. It has also suffered habitat loss due to ranching, cranberry farms, resorts, golf courses, housing developments, and invasion of trees. The lily is protected on some private and public lands, but remains endangered.

Where does it live? Narrow coastal areas of northern California and southern Oregon

Endangered status: Endangered (US Fish and Wildlife Service)

Xerosecta Giustii

This inch-long snail is found in only one part of Tuscany, Italy. It lives on land and breathes air with its one lung and four noses. Snails have a reputation for being slimy, but the mucus they secrete keeps them from drying out and helps them move.

Why is the *xerosecta giustii* important? It is slimy, slow, and not cuddly but, like all snails, it is very sensitive to changes in its ecosystem, serving as an early warning to humans. It is also an important source of food for birds, reptiles, and mammals.

Why is it in trouble? Habitat loss from agriculture and ranching, fires, and drought have decimated its population. Over one thousand snail species worldwide are classified as endangered. *Xerosecta giustii* is now bred in controlled environments in Tuscany to be reintroduced to prime habitats in the wild.

Where does it live? Tuscany, Italy

Endangered status: Critically endangered (IUCN)

Yellow-Eyed Penguin *Megadyptes antipodes*

The yellow-eyed penguin is quite colorful for a penguin. Besides the yellow eyes it was named for, it has a crown of yellow feathers and very pink feet. It only lives in New Zealand. The native Maori people call it, *Hoiho*, which means "noise shouter" because of its shrill call. The yellow-eyed penguin is shy, unlike other penguins, and it prefers to nest and hunt alone. It swims very fast and eats small fish and squid.

Why is the yellow-eyed penguin important? It is a warning sign for its habitat's health because it is highly sensitive to pollution, over-fishing, and climate change. This penguin also has quite a fan club and brings in money from tourism. And speaking of money, it is pictured on the New Zealand five-dollar note!

Why is it in trouble? Warmer oceans due to climate change mean less fish for it to eat. Other causes include getting caught in fishing nets, loss of nesting habitat, and high mortality of chicks due to dogs and cats. New Zealand is helping to safeguard its habitat with reserves, improving its ecosystem, and trapping mammal predators.

Where does it live? New Zealand

Endangered status: Endangered (IUCN)

Zanzibar Red Colobus *Piliocolobus kirkii*

This colorful monkey only lives in Zanzibar, an island off the coast of Tanzania in East Africa. Its tail is around two and a half feet long and usually longer than its body. The colobus uses its long tail to balance, its long legs to elegantly leap between trees, and its long fingers to grasp branches with ease.

The red colobus' diet is primarily young leaves, flowers, seeds, and unripe fruit—unlike other animals, it does not eat the sweeter ripened fruit. Its diet can cause stomachaches, but these monkeys have learned how to be their own doctors. Mother monkeys teach their little ones to eat charcoal to relieve the pain, and this knowledge is passed down through generations. They know to find charcoal from burned logs and tree stumps.

Why is the Zanzibar red colobus important? It is a good indicator of the health of its forest habitat. It eats vegetation and disperses seeds throughout the forest.

Why is it in trouble? Habitat loss due to deforestation, being eaten by humans and dogs, and being killed for causing crop damage have all played a role. Efforts are being made to protect the rain forest and its plants and animals like the colobus.

Where does it live? Zanzibar

Endangered status: Endangered (IUCN)

How You Can Help Endangered Species

- Learn about endangered species in your area. More information is found in the Bibliography at the end of this book.

- Visit and support wildlife refuges and parks. They provide safe habitats for many endangered species.

- Grow native plants in your yard to attract native pollinators like bees and butterflies. Minimize your use of pesticides, herbicides, and fertilizers.

- Put decals on your windows to prevent birds from flying into them and dying. This can save millions of birds each year.

- Reduce, recycle, and reuse. Donate items like old toys, clothes, and books to charities instead of throwing them away.

- Do not litter.

- Follow your local guidelines for handling unused paint and chemicals. If not disposed of properly, these can get into water sources and harm people and wildlife.

- Never buy anything made from any part of an endangered species, such as ivory, tortoise shell, or coral.

- Save energy. There are many ways to do this—from turning off lights when you leave a room, to installing solar panels in your home and ditching your car for a bike.

- Be vocal. Adults, vote for and support local, state, and national lawmakers who pass laws that support biodiversity and battle climate change.

- Adults and kids, learn all you can about how to help animals and plants in danger, and the impact of climate change on humans and all other living things. We are all in this together. We are all part of the living tapestry.

Bibliography

Asian Elephant

"Asian Elephant." Smithsonian's National Zoo, August 26, 2020. https://nationalzoo.si.edu/animals/asian-elephant.

"Asian Elephant." WWF. World Wildlife Fund. Accessed December 22, 2021. https://www.worldwildlife.org/species/asian-elephant.

Shah, Sunita. "The Remover of Obstacles." *The Jai Jais*. The Jai Jais, November 18, 2020. https://thejaijais.com/blogs/sunitas-blog/the-remover-of-obstacles.

Blue Whale

Fisheries, NOAA. "Blue Whale." NOAA. Accessed December 22, 2021. https://www.fisheries.noaa.gov/species/blue-whale.

Dewey, Tanya, and David L. Fox. "Balaenoptera Musculus (Blue Whale)." Animal Diversity Web. Accessed December 22, 2021. https://animaldiversity.org/accounts/Balaenoptera_musculus/.

Common Seahorse

Hashikawa, Micheleen. "Hippocampus Kuda (Common Seahorse)." Animal Diversity Web. Accessed December 22, 2021. https://animaldiversity.org/accounts/Hippocampus_kuda/.

Project Seahorse, July 26, 2021. https://projectseahorse.org/.

Dogwood

McGlone, Jim. "Dogwoods: Can Eastern Forests Function Without Them?" Fairfax County Virginia. Accessed December 22, 2021. https://www.fairfaxcounty.gov/soil-water-conservation/dogwoods-can-eastern-forests-function-without.

Pettis, Steve. "Native Dogwoods Mostly Gone in the Forest." NC Cooperative Extension News, July 21, 2021. https://henderson.ces.ncsu.edu/2021/03/native-dogwoods-long-gone-in-the-forest/.

Endangered Species Lists

"The IUCN Red List of Threatened Species." IUCN Red List of Threatened Species. Accessed December 22, 2021. https://www.iucnredlist.org/.

U.S. Fish and Wildlife Service/Endangered Species. Official Web page of the U.S. Fish and Wildlife Service. Accessed December 22, 2021. https://www.fws.gov/endangered/.

Ethiopian Wolf

"Ethiopian Wolf." African Wildlife Foundation. Accessed December 22, 2021. https://www.awf.org/wildlife-conservation/ethiopian-wolf.

Heimbuch, Jaymi. "The Last Wolves: Saving Africa's Rarest Carnivores." Earth Touch News Network, April 9, 2019. https://www.earthtouchnews.com/conservation/endangered/the-last-wolves/.

Florida Scrub-Jay

Arnold, Carrie. "The Key to Saving Florida Scrub-Jays May Run in the Family." *Audubon Magazine* Winter 2020, pages 22-29.

Terry, Mark. "Saving the Florida Scrub-Jay." Natural Resources Conservation Service. Accessed December 22, 2021. https://www.nrcs.usda.gov/wps/portal/nrcs/detail/national/newsroom/features/?cid=nrcseprd1367455.

Golden Frog

"Panamanian Golden Frog." Smithsonian's National Zoo, May 28, 2020. https://nationalzoo.si.edu/animals/panamanian-golden-frog.

Hawken, Paul Quore

"Paul Hawken Quotes." BrainyQuote. Xplore. Accessed December 22, 2021. https://www.brainyquote.com/quotes/paul_hawken_637124.

Hawksbill Sea Turtle

"Hawksbill Turtle." WWF. World Wildlife Fund. Accessed December 22, 2021. https://www.worldwildlife.org/species/hawksbill-turtle.

Ivory-Billed Woodpecker

Donahue, Michelle. "Possible Ivory-Billed Woodpecker Footage Breathes Life into Extinction Debate." *Audubon*, January 25, 2017. https://www.audubon.org/news/possible-ivory-billed-woodpecker-footage-breathes-life-extinction-debate.

Japanese Red-Crowned Crane

DeCarlo, Victoria. "Grus Japonensis (Red-Crowned Crane)." Animal Diversity Web. Accessed December 22, 2021. https://animaldiversity.org/accounts/Grus_japonensis/.

The Paper Crane Origami, March 15, 2017. https://thepapercraneorigami.com/.

Key Deer

Di Silvestro, Roger. "What's Killing the Key Deer?" National Wildlife Federation, February 1, 1997. https://www.nwf.org/Magazines/National-Wildlife/1997/Whats-Killing-the-Key-Deer.

Key Deer Protection Alliance. Accessed December 22, 2021. https://keydeer.org/.

Lemur

Baden, Andrea L. "Lemurs Are the World's Most Endangered Mammals, but Planting Trees Can Help Save Them." The Conversation, December 23, 2019. https://theconversation.com/lemurs-are-the-worlds-most-endangered-mammals-but-planting-trees-can-help-save-them-127878.

"Ring-Tailed Lemur." Smithsonian's National Zoo, October 3, 2019. https://nationalzoo.si.edu/animals/ring-tailed-lemur.

Mountain Gorilla

"5TF: 5 Things You Didn't Know about Mountain Gorillas (Gorilla Beringei Beringei)!" Dian Fossey Gorilla Fund, July 11, 2019. https://gorillafund.org/congo/5tf-mountain-gorillas.

"Mountain Gorilla." WWF. World Wildlife Fund. Accessed December 22, 2021. https://www.worldwildlife.org/species/mountain-gorilla.

Numbat

"Numbat." AZ Animals, February 16, 2021. https://a-z-animals.com/animals/numbat/.

Project Numbat, November 17, 2021. http://www.numbat.org.au/.

Ostrich

"Ostrich." African Wildlife Foundation. Accessed December 22, 2021. https://www.awf.org/wildlife-conservation/ostrich.

Polar Bear

Katz, C. "Polar Bears to Vanish from Most of the Arctic This Century." Eos, October 29, 2020. https://eos.org/articles/polar-bears-to-vanish-from-most-of-the-arctic-this-century.

"Polar Bear." WWF. World Wildlife Fund. Accessed December 22, 2021. https://www.worldwildlife.org/species/polar-bear.

Inspiration images courtesy Alan D. Wilson, Alamy.

Queen Alexandra's Birdwing

"Queen Alexandra's Birdwing." Swallowtail and Birdwing Butterfly Trust, May 11, 2020. https://www.sbbt.org.uk/the-birdwing-project/.

Rusty Patched Bumble Bee

"Fact Sheet: Rusty Patched Bumble Bee (Bombus Affinis)." Official Web page of the US Fish and Wildlife Service, May 29, 2019. https://www.fws.gov/midwest/endangered/insects/rpbb/factsheetrpbb.html.

"Rusty Patched Bumble Bee." Xerces Society. Accessed December 22, 2021. https://xerces.org/endangered-species/species-profiles/at-risk-invertebrates/bumble-bees/rusty-patched-bumble-bee.

Sea Otter

Allegra, J., R. Rath, and A. Gunderson. "Enhydra Lutris." Animal Diversity Web. Accessed December 22, 2021. https://animaldiversity.org/accounts/Enhydra_lutris/.

"Sea Otter." Defenders of Wildlife. Accessed December 22, 2021. https://defenders.org/wildlife/sea-otter.

Tiger

About. "Why Are Tigers Endangered? and What Can Be Done to Help." The Homeschool Scientist, November 5, 2021. https://thehomeschoolscientist.com/tigers-endangered/.

Gallagher, Katherine. "Types of Tigers: 3 Extinct, 6 Endangered." Treehugger, December 14, 2020. https://www.treehugger.com/endangered-types-of-tigers-5088803.

Utah Prairie Dog

Boyce, Andy, and Andrew Dreelin. "Ecologists Dig Prairie Dogs, and You Should Too." Smithsonian's National Zoo, February 23, 2021. https://nationalzoo.si.edu/conservation-ecology-center/news/ecologists-dig-prairie-dogs-and-you-should-too.

Moss, Laura. "9 Facts about Prairie Dogs." Treehugger, January 11, 2021. https://www.treehugger.com/things-you-didnt-know-about-prairie-dogs-4863942.

Venus Flytrap

"Venus Flytrap." U.S. Fish and Wildlife Service, September 1, 2021. https://www.fws.gov/southeast/wildlife/plants/venus-flytrap/.

Western Lily

"Western Lily." Official Web page of the California Department of Fish and Wildlife, June 24, 2014. https://wildlife.ca.gov/Conservation/Plants/Endangered/Lilium-occidentale.

Xerosecta Giusti

Platt, John R. "Snails Are Going Extinct: Here's Why That Matters." Scientific American Blog Network. Scientific American, August 10, 2016. https://blogs.scientificamerican.com/extinction-countdown/snails-going-extinct/.

"X Is for Xerosecta Giustii." Liz Brownlee Poet, May 24, 2014. https://lizbrownleepoet.com/2012/04/27/x-is-for-xerosecta-giustii/.

Yellow-Eyed Penguin

"Yellow-Eyed Penguin Trust - Dunedin, New Zealand." The Yellow-Eyed Penguin Trust, February 3, 2021. https://www.yellow-eyedpenguin.org.nz/.

"Yellow-Eyed Penguin Facts: New Zealand Wildlife Guide." WWF Natural Habitat Adventures. Accessed December 22, 2021. https://www.nathab.com/know-before-you-go/asia-the-pacific/new-zealand/wildlife-guide/yellow-eyed-penguins/.

Zanzibar Red Colobus

Shangari, Nina. "Zanzibar Red Colobus." New England Primate Conservancy, May 1, 2018. https://www.neprimateconservancy.org/zanzibar-red-colobus.html.

Inspiration image courtesy Alamy.

Vicki Malone was born and raised in Kansas and holds a bachelor of fine arts from the University of Kansas. Her love of plants and nature began in her grandmother's beautiful garden. She has lived on the East Coast for more than forty years, working as an editorial assistant, teacher, and artist. She currently lives with her husband in Chevy Chase, Maryland, and has three grown sons.

Vicki is a member of the American Society of Botanical Artists, Guild of Natural Science Illustrators, and Botanical Society of the National Capital Region. Her art has been shown at the Corcoran Museum of Art, Monticello Library, United States Botanic Garden, Delaware Art Museum, and galleries in the Washington, DC, area.

Her work has appeared in *Native Plants of the Mid Atlantic, America's Flora,* and the front and back covers of *Simple Gifts: Holidays at the White House 2010.*